I Think When I Am Older, I Might Be a Pharmacist!

Katrina Zearley

Dedication

To my friends and family who nurtured the future pharmacist in me; and to Francisca, who reminds me every day of why I might be a pharmacist.

I woke up feeling dizzy...
It's stuffy in my head.
I thought I had to go to school,
but mom and dad say "stay in bed!"

I'm getting up and ready,
and we're heading out the door.
My dad asks how I'm feeling…
I think my head is getting sore.

We get to the doctor's office
and they do a couple of tests.
They tell me that I must've caught the flu,
and that I need plenty of fluids and rest.

Then the doctor writes some scribble lines,
and says some big words I don't know.
But as soon as I know it, we're on our way,
and mom says we have one more place to go.

I peek outside my window,
I wonder where we might be?
My dad says we have to pick up my medicine,
inside the pharmacy.

The pharmacist sounds friendly,
very helpful and polite.
They're talking to someone about the "meds"
and that they should start taking them tonight.

Then I start to wonder what the pharmacist does...?
I know they work with pills and stuff,
but I thought I need to say no to drugs?

So I raise my hand up high,
just like I do in class.
I have so many questions for the pharmacist
I think it's about time I ask.

The pharmacist is very patient,
they listen to everything I say.
When I'm finally done, they smile,
and begin to answer away:

"What do you do in here all day?
What are all those bottles for?
Why do you wear that big white coat?
Why are there so many drug stores?"

"As your local pharmacist
I have a lot of chores.
I take care of hundreds of patients like you,
which is why there are so many stores."

"There are many different medicines
that all take care of many different things.
I know about every medicine on the shelves,
so, it just depends on what needs or troubles the next patient brings."

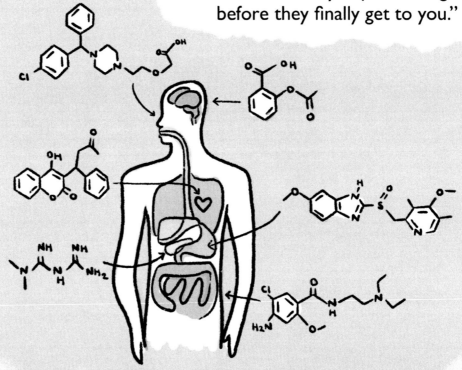

"I know all about the little things
that all of these drugs will do.
I make sure that they're just the right ones
before they finally get to you."

"And pharmacists wear a big
white coat
Because of history.
It helps us look professional,
and helps you to recognize me!"

"One of the many other things I do:
I double check your prescription ,
to make sure you get the right medicine
that was prescribed by your physician."

"Once your doctor writes a prescription
for the medication you need,
we can get you the right amount and bottle it up
so you can feel better, and life can proceed."

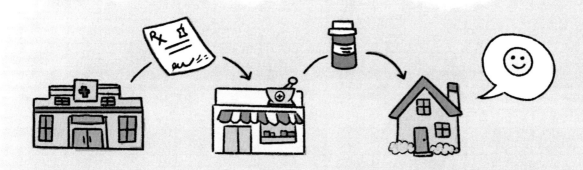

"There are plenty more tasks we do
as a part of the pharmacy routine.
Another thing I can do
is give you your vaccines!"

"Why are there medicines here,
but also over there?
Why are prescription medicines different?
How do they compare?"

"All the drugs you see back here,
are different than the rest.
You need a prescription from your doctor,
who knows what will work best."

"I learned a phrase or something in school,
and it's been made very clear...
If I'm suppose to say no to drugs,
what about all the ones in here?"

"You should say no to any drug
if they are not given by a doctor for you.
This will help keep you safe
and out of trouble, too."

"Sometimes I have heard people say
that medications cost too much
I don't really know what that means...
Is that that health insurance stuff?"

"Insurance is a big, big topic
that'll you'll probably learn about later.
But for now, it's important to know
that insurance can be a real money-saver."

"This job is like a quest,
a quest with many missions.
But I could not do it without the help
of the pharmacy technicians."

"The technicians help our patients, too,
and prepare their medications.
And while their job is just as important,
a pharmacist has to have more education."

"There are plenty of things you have to learn
in order to be a pharmacist, like me.
It does take a few extra years of school
to get a pharmacy degree."

While it takes a lot of knowledge
to be a pharmacist,
I think if you like math and science
you'll fit right in; I insist!"

"If you do end up liking pharmacy
there are actually many things you can do!
You'll know later on in life,
but just to name a few…

There are many different types of pharmacy,
besides "retail" stores like this.
There's hospital, and research, and big
pharmacy companies
that you probably didn't know exist!"

LAW + ACADEMIA

RESEARCH

PHARMACY

RETAIL

PHARMACEUTICAL MANUFACTURING

Rx
PHARMACY

COMPOUNDING

Pfizer

"BIG PHARMA"

INPATIENT + AMBULATORY + CLINICAL

33

While I'm learning lots of new things,
the rest of the pharmacy is hard-working and focused.
"What keeps the pharmacy so busy?" I ask.
Everyone is doing something different I notice.

"There are many other things
that we do in here all day.
We talk to doctors and patients on the phone
to make sure everything is going okay."

"We have to make sure that our patients
are taking their medicines.
Some people have to take theirs longer,
that's called a dosing regimen."

"You probably don't need to know that,
but it's one of the many things I do.
Keeping patients on track with their medications;
but since you're still so young, your parents or an adult will help you!"

"I know that there are big words I'm saying
that you might not understand.
Another job I have is to help people know
how to take the medicine when it's in their hands."

"The main goal of my job
is to make sure medications are used safe and well.
In addition, I can give you advice,
on which over-the-counter medicines are the best ones we sell."

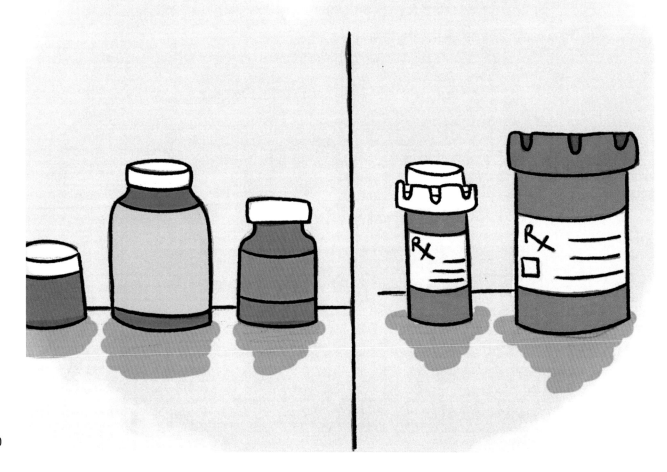

"Why are some medications *over*
instead of *behind* the counter?"

"Over-the-counter means the medication out there,
but the ones behind-the-counter have more power."

"All of the medications
on my side of the counter
are special treatment for the person who needs it
so, make sure to avoid any strange drugs you encounter!

Drugs that are over-the-counter
are also a treatment option.
Even though you don't need a prescription
you should still use them with caution!"

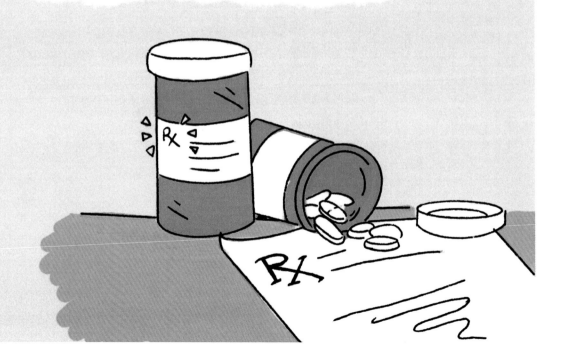

"You sure do know a lot!" I say.
"Do you like working here?"
"The job is definitely rewarding at the end of the day," they say,
so honest and sincere.

"Like any other job in healthcare it can be difficult, I'll admit.
But when you know you help so many people,
that's what makes the job worth it."

"The world needs plenty of us
who do what we do.
I hope I can convince you
to think about being a pharmacist too!"

A technician fills my medicine,
the pharmacist checks it again.
We pay and the pharmacist tells me its
special rules,
like how to take the medicine and when.

"Thank you for all your help!" I say.
"And for teaching me so much!"

"Of course, I hope you feel better!
And if you don't, please be in touch."

49

As I lay in bed that night,
I say goodnight to mom and dad.
They hope that I get well soon;
I know I will, and I'm glad.

I dream about all the things
that the pharmacist taught me today.
I don't know what I want to be when I grow up yet,
and for now, that is okay.

There is a lot that I still don't know,
about the big old grownup world…
But knowing that there are such cool jobs like that
gives my brain less of a whirl.

So, I take my medicine as directed,
still following the doctor's and pharmacist's special rules.
In a couple of days, I'm feeling normal,
and can get back to school!

Now I'm feeling better
and my flu will not be missed...
I think when I am older
I might be a pharmacist!

About the Author

Katrina Zearley is on her way to becoming a pharmacist, graduated with a BS in Pharmaceutical Sciences and a minor in Spanish at the University of Arizona ('22). She will continue her education at the University of Arizona's College of Pharmacy and will graduate with a PharmD in 2026. When not hard at work as a pharmacy technician, or deep in the books as a student, Katrina enjoys writing, drawing, listening to music, as well as spending time with friends and family (most likely teaching them pharmacy-related things).

Fun Fact! *Notice that the young girl and the pharmacist characters look alike? This was a personal ode to Katrina as a young child, inquisitive and curious about the pharmacy, and a future Katrina, a soon to be knowledgeable pharmacist.*

Made in United States
North Haven, CT
22 September 2023

41848310R00038